ILLUSTRATED SOCCER DICTIONARY FOR YOUNG PEOPLE

BY JAMES B. GARDNER

ILLUSTRATED

BY DAVID ROSS

PRENTICE-HALL, INC.
Englewood Cliffs, New Jersey

For my mother and father

Illustrated Soccer Dictionary for Young People
by James B. Gardner

Text copyright © 1976
by James B. Gardner

Illustrations copyright © 1976
by David Ross

Treehouse Paperback edition published 1978 by Prentice-Hall,
Inc. by arrangement with Harvey House, Publishers

Library of Congress Catalog Card Number 76-10044

Printed in the United States of America • J

ISBN 0-13-451146-8

10 9 8 7 6 5 4 3 2 1

Foreword

SOCCER is a fast-action, split-second, quick-thinking sport, accepted universally by over 100,000,000 dedicated fans as their Number One pastime. Except for the United States and Canada, soccer is *the* major sport in almost every country in the world.

Besides being the most popular, soccer is probably the oldest of all sports. No one can be sure of its origins, but historians have linked forms of soccer to the ancient Romans, Greeks, Egyptians, and Chinese.

Soccer, in some form, has been a constant companion to man throughout history. Most authorities recognize 1863 as the year when soccer had its beginnings as an organized sport. At this time a man named J. C. Thring drew up the laws of soccer, which were adopted by the London Football Association. The game was officially called Association Football. By 1888, it had been nicknamed "asoc." Soon "asoc" became "soccer."

Soccer's first excitement in the United States came in 1869 from New Brunswick, New Jersey, when Ivy League schools, Princeton and Rutgers, played a game with 50 players on a field measuring 360 by 225 feet. Before the game, the two captains got together and agreed that the goals would be eight paces apart. Running with the ball or throwing it would be illegal, as would any forms of tripping or holding. They also agreed that the game would end when ten goals were scored. After about four hours of play, Rutgers won with a score of 6 to 4.

Interest in soccer grew among other Ivy League schools with the establishment of teams at Yale and Columbia and with the formation of the American Intercollegiate Football Association in 1873. Despite the name, this association was interested in soccer, not football. And, contrary to popular belief, soccer did not develop from football; rather football was an offshoot of soccer and rugby. Today soccer is an integral part of most high school and college athletic programs.

Professional soccer in the United States got off to a promising, but complicated start in 1960, when a sports promoter named Bill Cox

formed the International Soccer League. Cox built his league by importing famous Latin American and European teams, which drew crowds from 15,000 to 25,000.

In attempting to expand the league, Cox ran into trouble with the United States Soccer Football Association, an organization sanctioned by the Federation Internationale de Football Association, the undisputed ruler in soccer. Instead of supporting Cox, the USSFA granted exclusive franchise rights to a group called the United States Soccer Association. At a cost of $25,000 a team, this group began to promote new clubs in 1967.

Meanwhile, Cox's International Soccer League merged with a second league to form an "outlaw" league called the National Professional Soccer League. With a $500,000 television contract from the Columbia Broadcasting System, the NPSL imported top players from around the world, attracting them with high salaries. In defiance of the Federational Internationale de Football Association, the NPSL formed teams and started play in ten cities across the United States.

This forced the United Soccer Association to beef up its programs in order to compete with the outlaw league. As a result, the United Soccer Association imported entire foreign

teams, with the approval from FIFA, and began league play with a ten-city schedule.

These events weakened instead of strengthened soccer as a professional sport in the United States. Each league had teams in the same six cities, resulting in low gate attendance and heavy financial losses.

Finally the two leagues merged to form the North American Soccer League. After several seasons of play, however, it became apparent that the multi-million dollar venture would end in failure. With five teams left in the NASL in 1969, most of them folded. Many of the foreign players, who made up a large part of the NASL, quietly returned home.

Late in 1969, the NASL began showing new signs of growth. Teams were added in several cities, including New York, and the league sponsored an International Cup Tournament. Its home teams were not expected to win over the powerful teams of Europe and Latin America, but the experience of playing against foreign soccer teams was invaluable.

Soccer has been an Olympic event since 1900 with Great Britain winning the greatest number of championships—three so far. The tiny country of Uruguay has won twice. By 1972 a United States soccer team was able to compete in the Munich Olympics. The team, composed of American All-Stars, did not get beyond preliminary matches, but its participation was a healthy sign for American soccer.

Professional soccer has continued to grow in the United States, with teams in twenty cities by 1975. The real impetus came in June of that year when the celebrated Brazilian athlete, Pele, signed a contract with the New York *Cosmos*. It guaranteed him an estimated 4.5 million dollars, for which he would play about 100 games over three seasons.

Pele has taught North Americans how dazzling and exciting soccer can be. His acquisition by the NASL helped open the door for a sound professional soccer program. This superstar has proved that it does not take a big man to be a soccer wizard. Pele is only 5'9" tall. Players of average size or even smaller are often standouts in soccer. Larger athletes

sometimes find it hard to follow the fast-paced action.

Soccer is a team sport, but each player is unique, having style and skills all his own. With eleven players on a side, it takes teamwork to win. Simply stated, the object of the game is to get the ball into the opponents' goal without using the hands or arms. One point is scored each time the ball is propelled through the goal.

Soccer equipment is minimal: jersey, shorts, shoes, knee socks, and a ball. The professional soccer season in the United States begins in April and ends in August. The college and high school seasons run from September to November.

A

A line formation—A practice formation where players line up in two lines facing each other.

Advancing from the goal—When an offensive player has maneuvered the ball past all defenders, a goalie has a better chance at saving a score if he comes out from the goal and directly challenges the offender. By doing this, the goalie can cut down the offensive player's angle of possibility, and reduce the chance for a score.

Advantage rule—This rule makes it possible for a team to continue playing after an infraction is called by the referee. A good referee will wave on a fouled player (if he can manage to continue), allowing him to continue play until it becomes apparent that the offensive team's chance for a score has been neutralized by the defensive team.

All Star game—A game played by two teams whose players are selected from various teams for their outstanding achievements and playing abilities.

Angle of possibility—A measure of the degree of difficulty of a player's shot on goal. The angle of possibility can be determined by drawing two straight lines from the ball, one to each goal post. The size of the angle determines a player's chances of scoring—the larger the angle, the better. Goalies study this aspect of soccer because it helps them to know where to position themselves for the greatest chance of stopping a shot.

Anticipation—A sixth sense. The ability of a player to sense another player's movements and adjust accordingly in intercepting passes, stealing the ball, stopping scoring drives and goals.

15

B

B line formation—A practice formation where players line up in two lines facing each other.

Back-up—A defensive term used when one player falls in behind a teammate to back his moves in defensive situations.

16

Ball—A soccer ball is spherical, having a circumference between 27 and 28 inches. The outer casing is usually leather, though a similar substance such as vinyl or rubber can be substituted, providing it is not injurious to players. The inflated ball should weigh between 14 and 16 ounces.

Ball in play—Except for going out of bounds, the ball is always in play, including rebounding from a goal post, crossbar, or corner flag post onto the playing field. It is considered in play during the time that an alleged rules' infringement occurs, until the referee makes a decision.

Ball out of play—The ball is out of play when it has completely crossed the touch line, goal line, or end line, regardless of its being on the ground or in the air.

Banana shot—A kick which requires a high degree of skill and accuracy. The banana shot is performed by striking the ball with the outside of the foot. When done correctly, the foot imparts a vicious spin to the ball, causing it to bend and dip in the air. The banana shot is difficult for a goalie to stop.

Blanket defense—A defense based on "numerical superiority" (more defensive players than opposing offensive players) and air-tight coverage in front of the goal mouth.

C

C line formation—A practice formation where players line up one behind the other, each player facing forward.

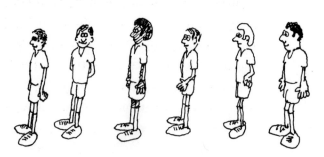

Captain of team—A player elected by each team, usually because of his leadership capabilities. He is the only member of the team allowed to discuss rule interpretations with the referee.

Center circle—A circle having a ten-yard radius which lies at the center of the playing field. During the kickoff, players of the team opposing the kicker must stay outside of this circle.

Center forward—Soccer's "goal-getter" is the possessor of a quick and powerful kick and the ability to head the ball into the net with consistency and accuracy. A skillful center forward can manipulate the ball through a band of defensive players, yet never hog the ball. Besides being able to lead an attack, he knows when to pass the ball to a team-mate who is in a better scoring position.

Center pass—A pass from the outside of the field to the center.

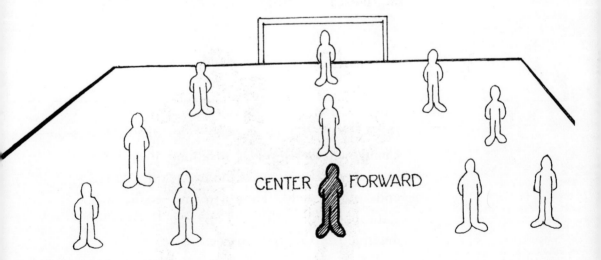

CENTER FORWARD

Center line—See *Half-way line.*

Center spot—A point marking the center of the playing field. The kick off is made from this mark at the beginning of each half.

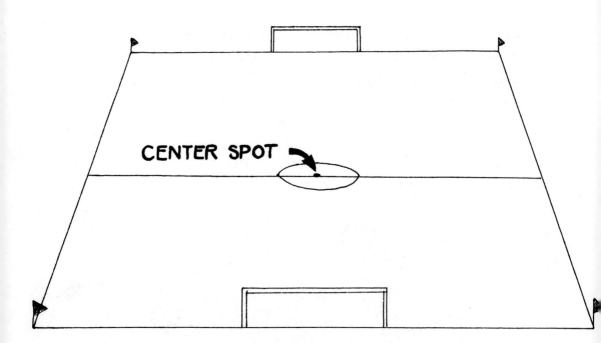

CENTER SPOT

Change of ends—When resuming play after regular or extra periods, the two teams change ends of the field. Thus a team's goalie will station himself in the goal opposite the one he defended in the previous period.

Change of pace—A technique for beating a defender while dribbling the ball. This deceptive skill requires the dribbler to move in at a moderate pace as close as possible to the defender and then, with a sudden burst of speed, accelerate past his opponent.

Charging—A technique used by a defensive player to steal the ball from an opposing player. The player runs and bumps the opposing player in an attempt to cause him to lose control of the ball. Charging in a violent or dangerous manner draws a penalty of a direct free kick for the other team. Charging can occur whether a player is in the air or on the ground.

Chest trapping—The means by which a player stops a kicked ball by using his chest to soften the impact of the ball and direct it to the ground where it can be quickly controlled.

Chest trap on a bouncing ball—A simple yet effective way of bringing the ball to a controlled stop on the ground. As the ball bounces up to a player, the upper part of the body is positioned well over the ball. Upon impact, the chest collapses, absorbing the impact, and allowing the ball to drop softly to the ground.

24

Chest trap on a fly ball—Similar to a chest trap on a bouncing ball. Upon impact, the body, formerly bent back and relaxed, is snapped forward to allow for a controlled rebound of the ball.

Chip pass—A kick that lofts the ball over short or long distances.

Circle formation—A practice formation where players form a circle with each man spacing himself at an equal distance between the two men on either side.

Clearing kick—A kick made by a player that sends the ball from one end of the field to the other, often changing a team's playing status from defensive to offensive.

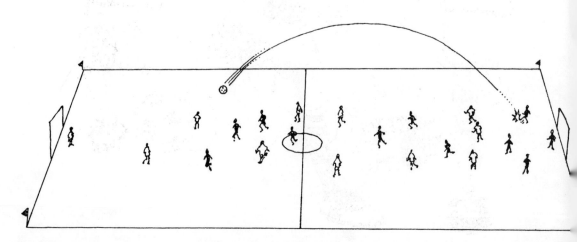

Club Championship of the World—Founded in 1960, this unofficial championship offers prestige for the winners of the European Cup and the South American Cup. It was designed to fill the four-year gap between World Cups.

Coaching area—An area designated for coaches' use, usually 20 yards in length, located five yards from, and parallel to, the touch lines on both sides of the playing field.

Combination—A play in which two offensive players team up for the purpose of outwitting an opponent.

Commit—To begin a movement, either defensively or offensively. An offensive player, who, by feinting, can draw a player out of position, has forced this player to commit himself.

Conditioning program—A series of training sessions consisting of fundamentals drills, scrimmages, exercises, and running, designed to get players in top physical condition.

Contain—To keep an opponent in a specific area.

Corner area—A quarter circle having a one-yard radius, located in each corner of the playing field.

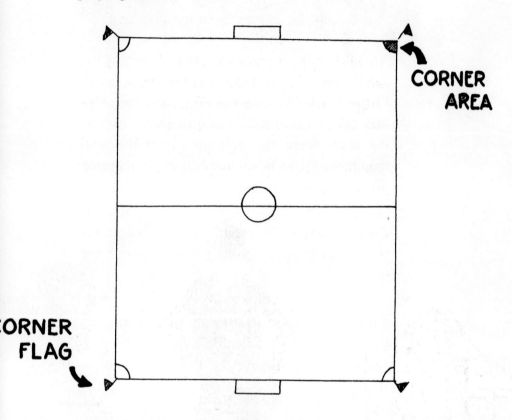

Corner flag—A bright-colored flag (usually red) about two feet long and one foot wide, attached to a pole five feet high and placed in each corner of the field. These flags help officials determine if a ball leaves the field by crossing the endline or the touch line.

29

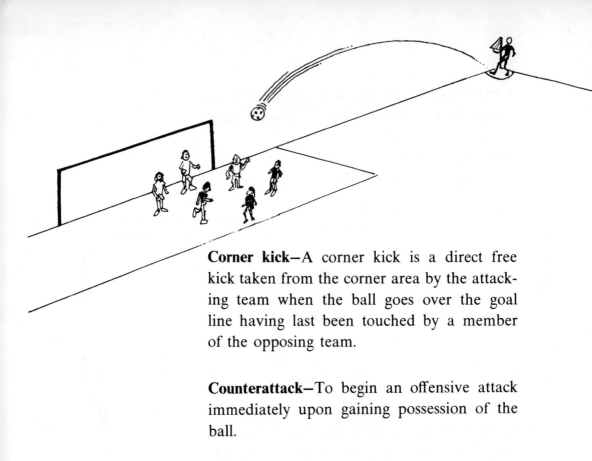

Corner kick—A corner kick is a direct free kick taken from the corner area by the attacking team when the ball goes over the goal line having last been touched by a member of the opposing team.

Counterattack—To begin an offensive attack immediately upon gaining possession of the ball.

Cover—The act of shadowing or guarding an opponent so that he can do nothing offensively, such as advancing the ball or passing or scoring.

Cross–A kick, commonly associated with the wings, from one side of the field to the other.

Crossbar–A wooden post fastened to the top of goal posts eight feet from the ground.

Cushioning–A trapping technique where the body is used to soften the impact of the ball.

D

Dangerous play—A play that a referee feels is unsafe or likely to result in an injury. The penalty is an indirect free kick.

Dead ball—A ball out of play. This includes a ball that has crossed an endline, touchline, or goal line, or after an infraction called by the referee, or when the referee stops play.

Deception—The ability to deceive or confuse another player to one's own advantage.

Decisive space—An expanse of field located in front of and around the goal.

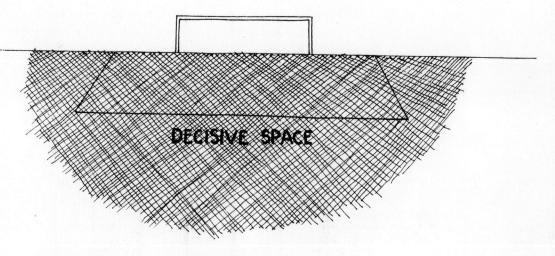

Decoy play—A team maneuver designed to draw one or more defending players out of their positions to allow for an easier scoring opportunity.

Defense—A term used to describe the team not in possession of the ball.

Defensive containment—Holding back an opponent in an attempt to gain possession of the ball.

Defensive screen—A defensive player, usually a halfback, whose job is to patrol the front of the defensive network and harass the opponents by marking the player in possession of the ball, intercepting passes intended for other penetrating forwards, and trying to force turnovers.

Direct free kick—A penalty kick (taken from the spot where the infraction occurs) awarded to one team when a member of the other team commits a personal foul. When awarded inside the penalty area, the ball is kicked from the penalty mark. All other players must stay outside the penalty area and at least ten yards from the ball. A goal can be scored directly from this kick.

PENALTY SPOT

Distribution—The goalie's actions in distributing the ball to his teammates. It is up to the goalie to get the ball to a well-placed teammate.

Diving pit—A practice aid used by many teams for the teaching of diving techniques. The diving pit is simply a pit filled with sand, sawdust, or foam rubber. Using it avoids nervousness and injury.

Drag—In an attempt to trap the ball, drag is pulling the ball with the foot in a desired direction.

35

Draw an opponent—To tempt a player to fall back from a position or a player he is guarding, so that the player he is covering will be free to receive a pass.

Dribbling—The means by which a player propels the ball in a desired direction by a series of short, controlled kicks.

Dribbling game—A practice game played with two teams of three or four players on a limited grid. The object of the game is to dribble the ball out of bounds while the other players attempt to stop you. There is no passing.

36

Drop ball—A drop ball situation occurs when a referee, holding the ball at waist level, releases it between any two opposing players, except the goalie. The ball must first hit the ground before it is played.

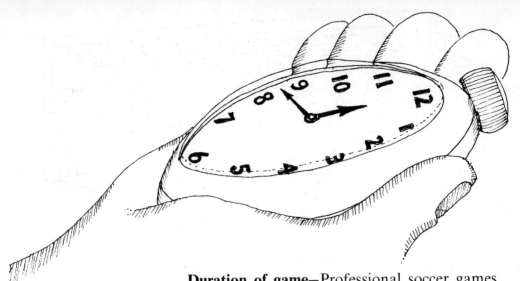

Duration of game–Professional soccer games are usually divided into two equal periods of 45 minutes, unless otherwise agreed upon. High school games are split into four equal periods of not more than 18 minutes each, or two halves of not more than 35 minutes each.

E

Endline (Goal line)–The boundary lines which mark each end of the playing field. The goal lines are considered part of the goal area they enclose.

ENDLINE
(GOAL LINE)

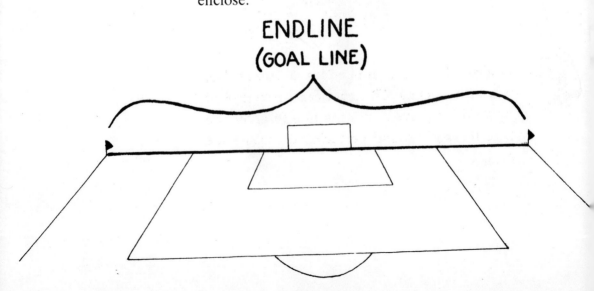

English—The spin applied to a soccer ball when it is kicked. This spin can be controlled by a skilled player, allowing him to hook and fade the ball around obstacles, especially the goalie.

English Football Association—This organization was formed in 1863, one year after the first ten rules of soccer were set up by an Englishman, J. C. Thring. These rules, with minor changes and additions, have remained in international use ever since. The EFA, which originally consisted of eleven clubs, now has 35,000 members spread out in 92 clubs in four divisions throughout England.

European Cup—Founded in 1956, this tournament is open to all teams of the European Union of Football Associations. With the exception of the World Cup, the European Cup is the most important title a European team can win. The counterpart of the European Cup is the South American Cup.

F

Fakes—Body movements employed to throw opposing players off balance and off guard.

Feints—See *Fakes*

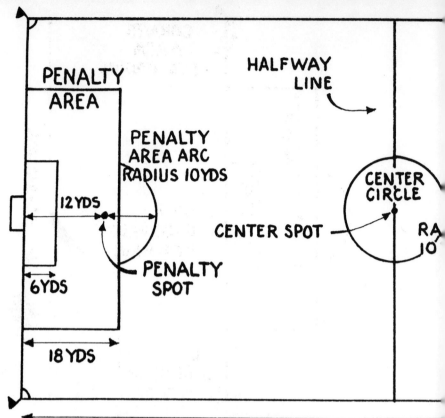

TOUCHLINE 100-130 YDS

Field of play—The soccer field is rectangular, 100 to 130 yards in length and 50 to 100 yards in width. The longer boundary, called the touchline, and the shorter boundary, called the endline, are distinctively marked and are considered part of the area they enclose. Corner flags mark each corner of the field. From each corner flag post a quarter circle is drawn, having a one-yard radius on the inside of the field. Midfield is marked by a center line and a center circle with a ten-yard radius. At each end of the field is the goal area,

42

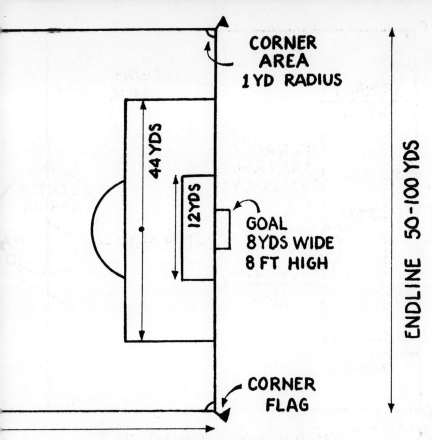

CORNER
AREA
1 YD RADIUS

44 YDS

12 YDS

GOAL
8 YDS WIDE
8 FT HIGH

ENDLINE 50-100 YDS

CORNER
FLAG

which extends six yards from the goal line and is 20 yards wide. The penalty area, which encloses the goal area, extends 18 yards from the goal area and is 44 yards wide. A penalty mark, two feet in width, is made 12 yards from and parallel to the goal line at a mid point in the field. From this line, penalty kicks are made. An arc of a circle having a ten-yard radius is described outside the penalty area, using the penalty mark as its center. Goals are placed on the center of each goal line and are eight yards wide and eight feet high.

Field vision—A developed skill that allows a player to see what is going on around him without letting opposing players know of his intentions.

First-time kick—Kicking the ball before it bounces.

Flags—These coaching aids can be used to mark zigzag courses, which players go through to improve feinting and dribbling skills.

44

Flick pass—A short deceptive pass to the side, made by pivoting the ankle into the ball. The flick pass is usually made while dribbling.

Formations—See Individual formations: *A formation, B line formation, C line formation, Circle formation, W formation, Zigzag formation.*

Free kick—See *direct* and *indirect free kick.*

Free-lance offense—A type of offense that uses no set plays or strategies. Most coaches agree that this type of play should be limited to those teams possessing above-average talent.

Freezing the ball—A method of retaining possession of the ball without attempting to advance it into the opponents' half of the field. This type of stalling is sometimes used by teams when they are ahead by only one or two goals. The object is to keep the ball away from the opposing team so it can't get a chance to score.

Fullbacks—The fullback is, above all, a defender. He strives to instill confidence in his teammates by giving them the feeling that he alone can break up a scoring drive. He must possess and display an even-tempered style of play. This includes consistency in tackling techniques, an ability to recover quickly if outwitted, and the skill to function effectively when the pressure is on.

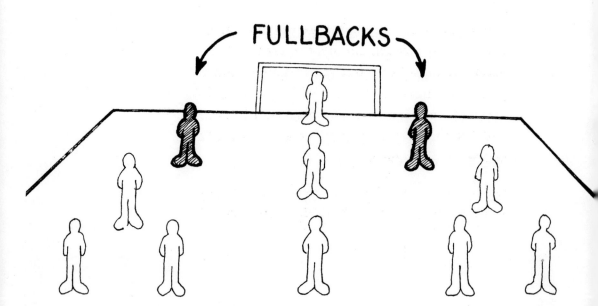

FULLBACKS

Fundamentals—Fundamentals in soccer are kicking, dribbling, passing, heading, trapping, and tackling.

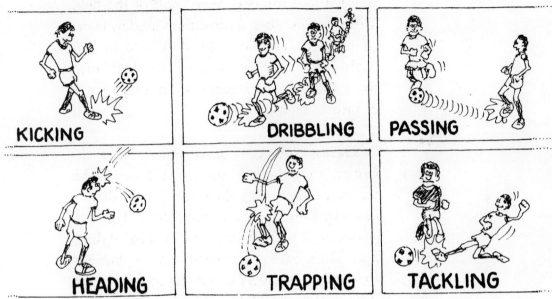

KICKING

DRIBBLING

PASSING

HEADING

TRAPPING

TACKLING

G

Game plan—A system of strategies and tactics compiled by a coach and his players which the team attempts to follow in a game. Game plans vary in order to deal with specific situations such as dangerous players, offensive and defensive styles of play, or an opponent's known performance.

Garter—An elastic band or suspender worn by some soccer players to hold up their socks.

47

Give and go—See *Wall pass*

Goal—A goal is scored when the ball completely crosses the goal line, passing within the goal posts and the crossbar.

Goal area—The goal area lies inside the penalty area directly in front of the goal. It measures twenty yards long by six yards wide.

GOAL AREA

PENALTY AREA

Goal kick—A kick taken by the defending team from the goal area when the ball crosses the goal line (not into the goal), having last been touched by a member of the opposing team.

Goalkeeper (Goalie)—The goalie stations himself in front of the goal. It is his job to keep the ball out of the goal. He is the only player who is allowed to touch the ball with his hands or to advance it within the penalty area by bouncing it between steps. A good goalie possesses a sure set of hands, powerful kicking legs, and the ability to come up with a game-winning save when the pressure is on.

GOALIE

Goal nets—The vinyl or rope mesh which is attached to the goal posts and crossbar. Goal nets are used principally so that there is no mistake made about whether a goal is actually scored or not. The nets slope out from the back of the goal at a 45 degree angle.

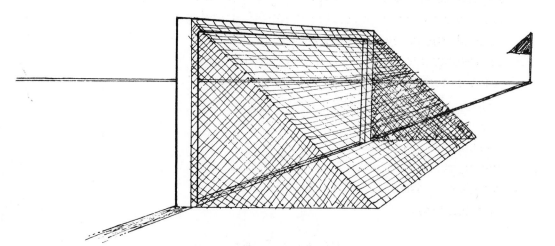

Goal posts—Goal posts are placed in the center at each end of the playing field, eight yards apart. They are usually made of wood, 4 × 4 inches in thickness, and eight feet high.

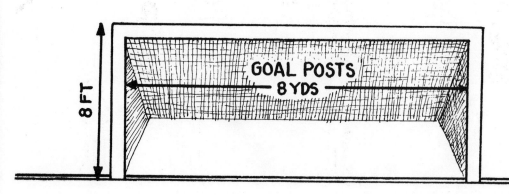

Grid—A specific area of the playing field used in practice situations to simulate the confined spaces in which a player must work.

H

Halfbacks—Most soccer experts agree that the team which can control the midfield usually controls the game. The halfbacks are the players responsible for the action at midfield. They must excel in all the fundamental abilities of soccer. Halfbacks are the connecting links between the fullbacks and the forwards. They constantly strive to get and keep the ball from the opposing team and to set up their forwards by passing, kicking, heading, tackling, and thinking.

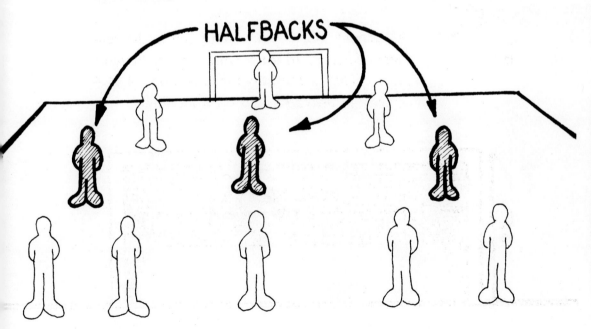

HALFBACKS

Half-time—The interval between the two playing periods where players rest and discuss game tactics and strategy with their coaches. This period lasts 15 minutes.

Half-volley kick—A kick made just after the ball bounces from the ground. A well-executed, half-volley kick results in a hard low drive.

Half-way line—The half-way line is a chalked line which runs parallel to the goal line, dividing the playing field in half.

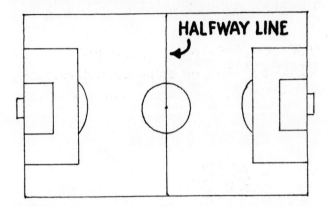

Handling—Intentionally handling the ball with the hands or arms is illegal. Using hands or arms to protect the body is also illegal. The penalty is a direct free kick for the other team. Unintentional handling, which happens when the ball strikes the arms or hands, is legal and is indicated by the referee's signal and vocal call, "play on."

Headband—A cloth band (usually terry cloth) is worn by many soccer players. It aids in cushioning the head when heading the ball, keeps perspiration off the forehead, and keeps hair out of the players' eyes.

Heading—The technique of using the flat, center part of the forehead to propel a ball in midair.

Head-on tackle—The technique of stealing the ball from an opposing player by meeting him head-on and holding the ball with one foot or wedging it with both feet. When contact with the ball is made, the player attempting to make the tackle should throw a shoulder block to try to upset the other player's balance. The ball should then be slid clear of the opponent.

Heeling—A pass or kick in which the heel of the foot is used to propel the ball.

Holding—It is illegal for a player to hold an opponent with his hands or arms. The penalty awarded is a direct free kick.

Hooking—Using the outstretched leg and foot to deflect a ball from an opponent to a team-mate.

I

Indirect free kick—A free kick awarded to one team when a member of the other team commits an illegal action. The kick is taken from the spot of the infraction. A goal cannot be scored directly from this kick.

Indoor soccer—A scaled-down version of regular soccer, usually played in a gymnasium. The number of players is reduced from eleven to five, six, or seven. The size of the goal is reduced to about fifteen by five feet.

57

Inside forward—Top physical condition, quick thinking, speed, and accuracy in ball handling are only a few of the qualities of a good inside forward. He is the one who must get the ball from his halfbacks and "feed" it to his wings or center forward. The inside forward must constantly be on the alert to set up a score. Offense is not the only thing on the inside forward's mind. He is always ready to help his halfbacks overcome the opposition on defense.

Inside-of-the-foot dribble—A maneuver where the ball is propelled by tapping it alternately with the inside of each foot. This type of dribbling allows the ball to be moved in a fast and controlled manner.

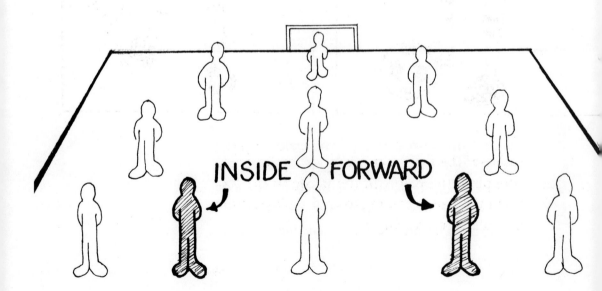

INSIDE FORWARD

Inside-of-the-foot kick—With the body facing straight ahead, this kick is made by striking the ball with the inside of the foot. The hip and knee of the kicking foot are bent during impact as if one were crossing his legs.

Inside-of-the-foot trap—A way of trapping (stopping) the ball with the inside of the foot when the ball is coming toward a player from the side or on an angle.

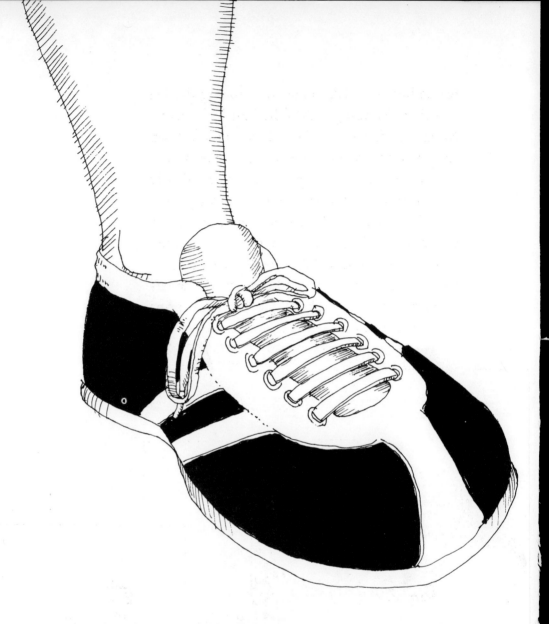

Instep—The part of the foot most often used in kicking a soccer ball. The instep is located on the top of the foot, and is covered by the laces of a soccer shoe.

Instep kick—A kick made by swinging the leg and then snapping it into the ball by straightening it at the knee. The toe is pointed down and in. Contact with the ball is made on the laces of the shoe. The grounded leg is slightly bent during impact. In following through, the toe of the kicking foot is still pointed down and relaxed. The head and eyes are pointed down as the grounded foot begins to straighten and then leaves the ground to allow for maximum power. Throughout the kick, the arms are positioned out to the sides for balance.

Inswinger ball—A ball that curves in toward the goal following a corner kick. The curve results from a spin the foot gives the ball.

Interception—The legal means by which a defensive player steals the ball while it is being passed from one offensive player to another.

STEAL

Interval training—A type of training where an athlete runs a specific distance at high speed followed by a rest period of the same time interval or less. The run-rest series is repeated ten times. The theory is to get the heart beating rapidly without allowing it to recover. Many coaches believe this to be an excellent training technique.

Isometric training—A type of training exercise in which the athlete pushes against an immovable object (such as a wall) with his arms, exerting maximum pressure for seven seconds. By repeating this process many times, the athlete develops stronger arm muscles, which are very important in soccer. Other isometric exercises strengthen muscles in other parts of the body.

Isotonic training—A type of conditioning where a player repetitively lifts heavy weights to build up strength and endurance.

J

Jersey—A jersey, or shirt, is part of the required soccer uniform. Almost all jerseys have numbers on them for identification purposes. When choosing a jersey, players should find one that allows freedom of movement and comfort.

Jockeying—A stalling maneuver in which a defensive player attempts to delay an offensive forward's progress by guarding him very closely.

Juggling—The art of keeping a soccer ball in the air by using any part of the body except the arms or hands. Practice at juggling will develop a player's sensitivity for, and coordination with, the ball.

Jump kick—A kick performed by jumping into the air while swinging either leg into the ball.

Jumping (at an opponent)—Jumping at an opponent is illegal, and a direct free kick is awarded to the opposing team. Jumping into the air to *play* the ball is perfectly legal.

K

Keep-away game—A game in which one team attempts to win by keeping the ball from the other team.

Kick to a spot—Kicking the ball to a spot where a teammate can drive in and dribble it without breaking stride.

Kickboard—Also called a rebound board. A kickboard is used to develop a soccer player's fundamental skills. Players can practice by themselves simply by kicking at the board and waiting for the rebound. Kicking and trapping techniques can be mastered with a minimum of wasted time.

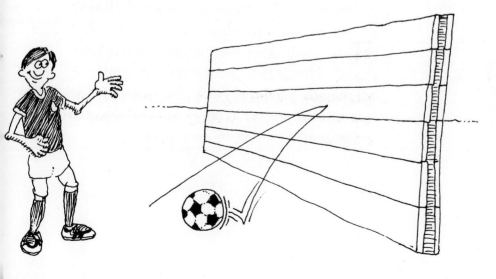

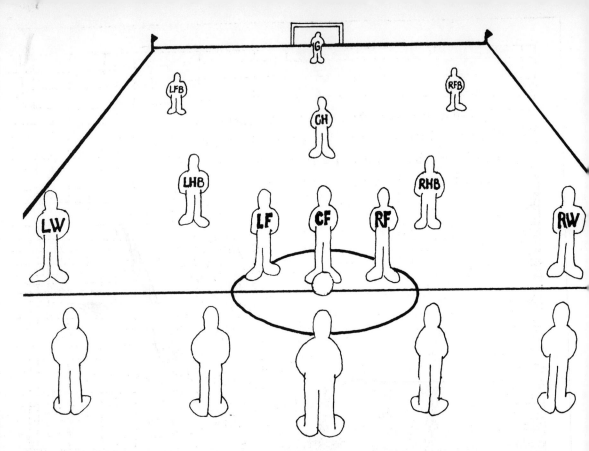

Kick off—Every soccer game is started by a player taking a place kick from the center spot into his opponents' half of the field. Every player must remain in his own half of the field until the ball is kicked and has moved at least the distance of its circumference (27 inches). Players of the opposing team must stay at least 10 yards from the ball until it has been kicked. (Hence the center circle.) A goal may not be scored directly from a kick off. The kick off takes place after each goal is scored and at the beginning of each period.

68

Kicking at the ball when held by the goalie—A direct free kick is awarded to a team if a member of the other team kicks or attempts to kick the ball when the goalie is holding it.

Kicking (an opponent)—Kicking or attempting to kick an opponent is illegal. The penalty is a direct free kick for the other team.

L

Lead pass—Similar to kicking to a spot. A player makes a pass beyond a teammate so he can pick it up without losing speed.

Leg trap—A trap where the leg is used to bring the ball to a controlled stop. The leg should be held at such an angle that the ball, when hitting it, will be deflected softly to the ground in front of the player.

Length of periods—See *Duration of game.*

Linesmen—Two linesmen assist the referee by indicating: 1. offside; 2. when the ball is out of play; 3. which team is entitled to a corner kick or throw-in.

Linkmen—These players are also called midfielders or halfbacks. They are the links between the forwards and the fullbacks.

Loft—A kick in which the ball is lifted high into the air. The loft is usually made in an attempt to get the ball over the heads of nearby defensive players.

Long passing game—A method of offense based on long, accurate passes.

M

Magnetic board—A metal board which uses magnetic figures to illustrate soccer strategies such as plays and diagrams.

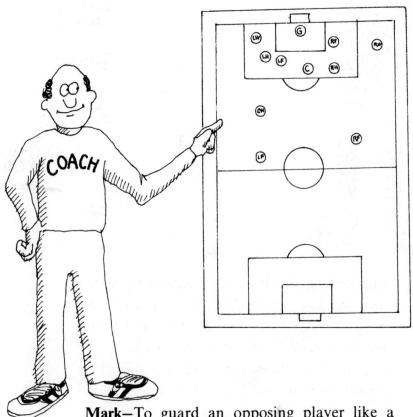

Mark—To guard an opposing player like a shadow.

Misconduct—A player who repeatedly shows unsportsman-like conduct, who repeatedly infringes on the rules, or who balks at the referee's decisions will first be cautioned by the referee. The referee can disqualify him if he persists in misconduct or if he exhibits violent conduct such as abusive language. (See *Yellow card.*)

73

Mud—Mud, along with other wet field conditions, plays an important part in soccer. Poor footing can rob a good defender of speed and agility. An experienced offensive forward can easily leave an inexperienced defender lying on the ground in the mud. Apart from body control, a muddy field also affects ball control. A short passing game is difficult to play in mud, for the ball can stop suddenly in a puddle. Moving the ball through the air is a better way to play when wet conditions prevail. The goalie must take special and deliberate care during wet weather, for a muddy ball is slippery and hard to handle.

N

National Soccer Coaches Association of America—A group composed of soccer coaches and anyone else interested in soccer. Through its quarterly publication, *Soccer Journal,* and its annual convention, the NSCAA contributes to the development of the game and the professional improvement of coaches.

Negative passing—An unwillingness to take risks in order to advance the ball, or an overly cautious manner when advancing the ball. As an example, a team using this strategy may have one of its forwards pass the ball backwards, when the logical move would be to advance the ball.

Net-minder—Another term used to describe a goalie.

Nine major fouls—Handling the ball, holding, pushing, or striking an opponent, charging violently, charging from behind, tripping, kicking, and jumping at an opponent are the nine major fouls in soccer. When a referee calls a player for one of these violations, he awards

76

a direct free kick to a member of the opposing team. When a violation is committed by a member of the defensive team inside his own penalty area, a direct free kick is taken by the opposing team from the penalty spot. (See *Penalty kick*)

North American Soccer League—An organization formed in 1968 as a result of the merger between the United Soccer Association and the National Professional Soccer League.

O

Obstruction—A deliberate act by a defensive player who uses his body as an obstacle to keep an opponent from getting possession of the ball. The penalty is an indirect free kick.

Offense—The team in possession of the ball.

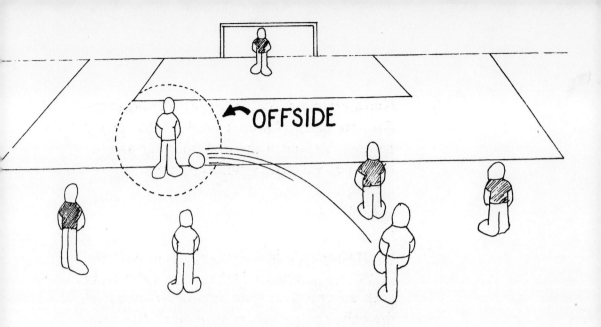

OFFSIDE

Offside—A player is considered offside unless there are two opponents between him and the goal he is attacking. A player cannot be offside if he is in his own half of the playing field. During goal kicks, corner kicks, and drop ball situations, a player can never be offside. As long as the ball is between a player and the goal he is attacking, he does not need to worry about being offside.

Outside forward (wing)—A good wing is known for his ability to get possession of the ball, move it speedily and deceptively downfield, and "feed" it to his other forwards who are in scoring positions. He must have stamina, good feet, and a good head. The two wings are always ready to harass opponents when their team is on the defensive.

79

Outside-of-the-foot dribble— A maneuver whereby the ball is propelled forward by alternately tapping it with the outside of each foot. The foot should be turned in, pigeon-toed fashion. Contact with the ball is made with the area around the little toe.

Outside-of-the-foot trap—A difficult and deceptive maneuver where the outside of the foot is used to stop an oncoming ball and deflect it in a desired direction.

Outside left—The left outside forward.

Outside right—The right outside forward.

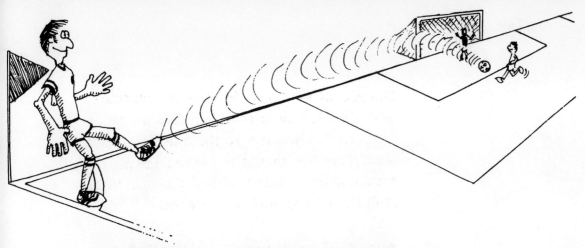

Outswinger ball—A ball which curves away from the goal (during a corner kick) as a result of the spin imparted to it upon impact. This shot is often considered an offensive advantage because the ball swings away from the goalkeeper toward incoming forwards, which provides greater impact for a kick or header. It sometimes tempts a goalkeeper to come out from the goal, leaving him in a defensively weak position.

Over-arm throw—A toss by the goalie which, when properly executed, sends the ball accurately over long distances.

Overhead volley—A kick made by allowing the top half of the body to fall backwards while swinging the kicking foot off the ground with the non-kicking foot following. The palms should be face down, ready to break the fall. Contact with the ball is made at about shoulder height, with a quick snap of the knee, toes pointing back to the shin. This type of kick is extremely effective for catching a goalie off guard. It should be attempted only by experienced players.

82

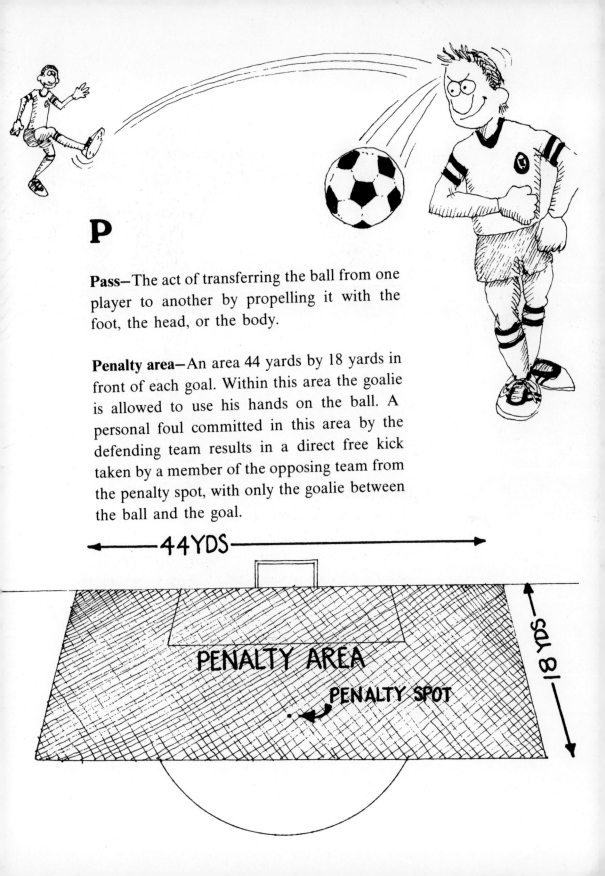

P

Pass—The act of transferring the ball from one player to another by propelling it with the foot, the head, or the body.

Penalty area—An area 44 yards by 18 yards in front of each goal. Within this area the goalie is allowed to use his hands on the ball. A personal foul committed in this area by the defending team results in a direct free kick taken by a member of the opposing team from the penalty spot, with only the goalie between the ball and the goal.

←—44YDS—→

PENALTY AREA

PENALTY SPOT

18 YDS

Penalty kick—See *Direct and Indirect free kick.*

Penalty arc—An arc of a circle, using the penalty spot as its center, and having a ten-yard radius. The penalty arc rests on the penalty area and is a restraining line for penalty kicks.

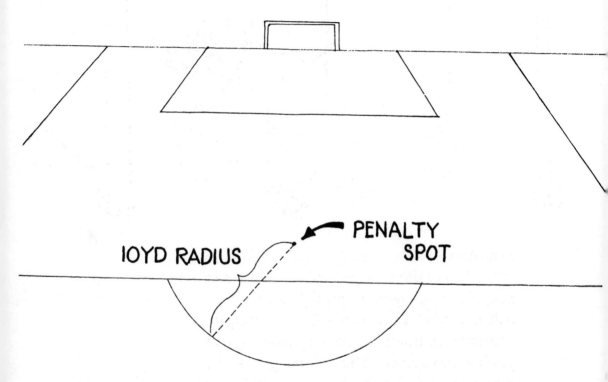

Penalty spot—A mark, two feet in length, located in the center of the penalty area at a point 12 yards from the goal line. Penalty kicks are taken from this line.

Pendulum ball—A special soccer ball, like a tether ball, which is attached to a string and hung from an overhead pipe. The pendulum ball is helpful to players who are trying to improve their heading, volleying, shooting, and passing techniques. The advantage of the pendulum ball is that players can kick and head the ball without having to chase it.

Penetration—The act of moving the ball well into the opponents' half of the field.

Pigeon holes—The two upper corners of each goal, which are almost impossible for the goalie to defend. A shot aimed accurately at the pigeon holes is almost a sure score.

Pitch—A British term for "playing field."

Pivot kick—A kick performed by swinging the kicking leg from the hip in a sweeping, circular motion while the grounded foot is pivoted in the direction of the intended flight of the ball. Contact with the ball is made with the instep; the toe is pointed down and inward.

Place kick—A kick at the ball while it is stationary on the ground.

Placing hands on an opponent—A direct free kick is awarded to one team if a member of the other team places his hands on an opponent in an effort to gain possession of the ball.

Playmaker—A player who concerns himself with the ever-present possibility of setting up plays which result in scores. This player accomplishes his "goal" by feeding his teammates with well-placed passes.

Portable goals—Soccer goals which are light in weight, adjustable in size, and sturdy in construction. These practice units are versatile where space is limited.

Positioning—The spot where a goalie stands in the goal. (See *Angle of possibility*.)

Positive passing—The willingness of a coach to direct his players to pass the ball through strong defensive barriers, to be aggressive and opportunistic.

89

Power play—An intense attack by the offense designed to keep the defensive pinned down and unable to break out. Under the constant pressure of attack, the team in possession can often "crack" a defense and send the ball into the net for a score.

Pressure defense—A harassing type of defense which attempts to force the offensive team to make mistakes which lead to turnovers.

Pulling the book—(See *Yellow card*) A referee's way of letting a player know that he is guilty of misconduct. The referee pulls out a little black book and writes the player's name down. Three times and he's out!

Punching—A defensive action performed by goalies to block a high shot on goal.

Push pass—A pass made by swinging the kicking leg at the ball from the hip in the desired direction of the pass. Contact is made with the inside of the foot. The push pass is used when a short, accurate pass is wanted.

Pushing—Pushing a player with the hands or extended arms is an illegal movement. The penalty is a direct free kick.

R

Reading the game—The ability to observe and interpret important fundamental characteristics of the opposing team and adjust one's own style of play accordingly.

Rebound—The "returning" action of a ball when it hits a solid object.

Referee—One referee is appointed for each match. He is responsible for controlling the game, and his word is law. (In high school and college soccer, two referees with equal jurisdiction are used.)

REFEREE INDICATING FOOT OVER THE SIDE-LINE ON THROW-IN

Retreating funnel defense—A defensive maneuver in which the defensive players fall back into their own half of the field while relying on the principle of delay. The forwards and the halfbacks constantly strive to bottle up the offense in an attempt to give their teammates a chance to set up and properly deal with the oncoming attack.

S

Save—A defensive maneuver performed by a goalie or his teammate which prevents the ball from entering the goal.

Score—The record of goals scored in a match. One point is awarded for each goal.

Scorer—The official in charge of keeping score.

Screening—Temporarily positioning the body between an opponent and the ball in an attempt to draw the opponent out of position.

95

Scrimmage—A practice game between two teams. Play is often stopped to allow coaches to discuss techniques and plays with players.

Scrimmage vest—Multi-colored vests worn by players in a scrimmage for identification purposes.

Second touch shot—A developed skill in which a player deflects an oncoming ball in such a direction that he can immediately take a shot on a goal. This shot is extremely effective in catching a goalie off guard.

Shepherding—A maneuver in which a defensive player gives ground to an offensive player who has the ball, with the objective of getting the offensive player to move in a specific direction.

Shin guards—Protective pads worn by many players between the sock and the shin.

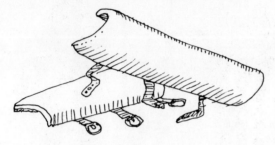

Shoes—Most soccer shoes have leather uppers and molded soles. Cleats or studs are permitted as long as they are no more than one-half inch in diameter or in length.

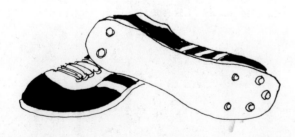

Shooting—The act of kicking the ball at the goal.

Shooting tee—A practice device useful in developing a player's volleying, passing, and shooting abilities. It serves the same purpose as a golf tee.

Short passing game—A method of offense based on short, accurate passes.

Shorts—Part of the required uniform. Most players choose loosely fitting cotton shorts to allow free movement and comfort.

Six-man soccer—A variation of regular soccer, in which there are only six players on a side: a goalie, two backs, and three forwards. Six-man soccer gives young players more opportunities to handle the ball and practice the skills taught in drills.

Sliding tackle—A desperation attempt to gain possession of the ball. A defensive player slides on the ground, using an extended leg to knock the ball from an opposing player to the tackler's teammates.

Soccer signals—

GOAL

PLAY ON

HANDLING THE BALL

TRIPPING

STRIKING

JUMPING

OFFSIDE

HOLDING

CHARGING VIOLENTLY
CHARGING - BEHIND

PUSHING

DANGEROUS PLAY

GOALKEEPER
CARRYING BALL

DEAD BALL

TIME OUT

UNSPORTSMANLIKE
CONDUCT

INDIRECT
KICK

OBSTRUCTION

CORNER KICK

DIRECT KICK

Sole-of-the-foot pass—A deceptive maneuver performed by placing the sole of the foot lightly on the ball and pulling it backwards.

Sole-of-the-foot trap—A method of stopping a ball that is coming toward a player on the ground or at a low angle. By timing the exact arrival of the ball, the sole of the foot is used to wedge it to a standstill where it can be played in a controlled manner.

Solo—An attempt to score without help from a player's teammates.

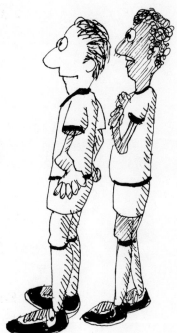

Space—A term used to describe an area of the field (the area around the goal) that the offensive team constantly strives to control, while the defensive team tries to keep control of it, too.

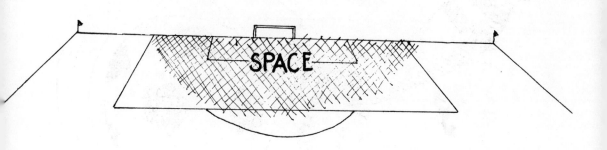

LW LF CF RF RW

Spearhead formation—An attacking formation led by the center forward with support from both inside forwards. The two wings work to draw the defensive fullbacks away from the goal area and then try to get the ball to the center and inside forwards.

Square pass—A pass directly across the field to a man moving forward.

Staleness—A term used by many coaches to describe a player who is having a slump in his performance.

Stanley Matthews' Magic—Stanley Matthews, a great wing player for Blackpool, England, used his exceptional speed and perfect timing to consistently beat over-anxious fullbacks down the sideline. His ability to outwit defenders by holding back his move until the last second was so widely known and used that it became known as "Stanley Matthew's Magic."

Stomach trap—A maneuver used to control a bouncing ball. A player leans out over the oncoming ball and uses his stomach to deflect it to the ground.

Stop and go—A popular technique used by dribblers who are being closely pursued by an opponent. The ball handler pretends to continue straight ahead; instead he stops completely and suddenly by placing the sole of the foot on the ball, feints one way, and accelerates in another direction. This technique will often prove successful in shaking off an over-anxious defender.

Stopper—The defenseman who plays in the area of the field near the center and in front of the penalty area, usually the center half-back.

Strikers—Also called forwards. See individual forward positions.

Striking—Striking or attempting to strike an opponent is illegal and draws a direct free kick for the other team.

Style of play—The type of game that a team plays on an individual and group basis, such as a long or short passing game, hustling and aggressive play, or slow and determined action.

Substitutes—In high school and college, a soccer team may substitute as many players as it wishes between periods when a goal has been scored, when the ball goes over the endline, or when a player has been disqualified. At the professional level, soccer teams are usually limited to two or three substitutions a game. These substitutions may take place during the same times as in high school and college play.

Sudden reverse—A technique where the dribbler shows all intentions of moving straight ahead but instead stops the ball with the sole of his foot, changes direction, and dribbles away from his opponent.

Support—The act of playing near the ball in order to have greater strength in controlling it.

Swiss bolt—A style of soccer that allows five attackers and five defenders plus a reserve defender called the "bolt".

Switch—When a player leaves his normal position, a teammate will often switch positions to cover for him.

T

Tackling—The technique of stealing the ball from an opposing player by using the feet to deflect or control the ball.

Talking it up—A psychological method of beating an opposing team by constantly communicating with other members of your team on the field.

Team—A typical soccer team consists of a coaching staff, trainers and physicians, equipment managers, and many players. The coach, however, can field only eleven players for a match. They are the center forward, left and right inside forwards, left and right outside forwards (wings), center halfback, left and right halfbacks, left and right fullbacks, and the goalkeeper. Each team has a captain, who is the only one permitted to discuss rule interpretations with the referee.

Teamwork—Playing together as a unit.

110

Thigh trap—A method of bringing the ball to a controlled stop by using the inner or outer portion of the thigh to deflect it to the ground. Upon impact, the thigh should "give" slightly so the ball does not bounce wildly away.

Throw-in—A throw-in is a two-handed, overhead pass made with both feet on the ground from the point where the ball crosses the touchline. The throw-in is awarded to the opponents of the team that last touched the ball before it went out of bounds.

SIDELINE

Timekeeper—The official responsible for keeping track of playing time, including time-out periods.

Time-out—An interval of time when the clock is stopped following the scoring of a goal or by order of a referee.

Torpedo header—This term was coined because the player performing this difficult maneuver resembles a torpedo. The player dives at the ball and heads it in the same manner as a normal head shot.

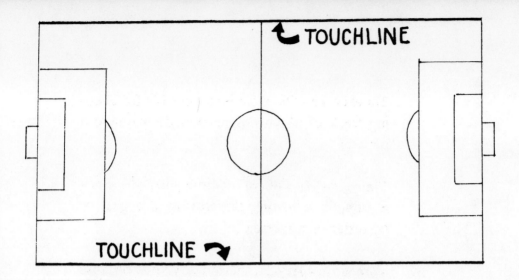

TOUCHLINE

TOUCHLINE

Touchline—The boundary lines which parallel each side of the playing field. The touchlines are usually marked with lime or chalk and are considered part of the area they enclose.

Trapping—Gaining controlled possession of the ball that is coming at a player by using any part of the body except the hands or arms.

Tripping—Any means by which one player attempts to trip or cause an opponent to fall or lose his balance is illegal. The penalty is a direct free kick.

Turnover—Change in possession of the ball from one team to another.

U

United States Soccer Football Association—This governing body reigns supreme over all professional and amateur soccer organizations in the United States. It also governs international tournaments and the National Amateur Challenge Cup, National Challenge Cup, and the National Junior Cup. The USSFA has been a member of the Federation Internationale de Football Associations since 1914.

V

Volleying—Kicking a ball without trapping or stopping it.

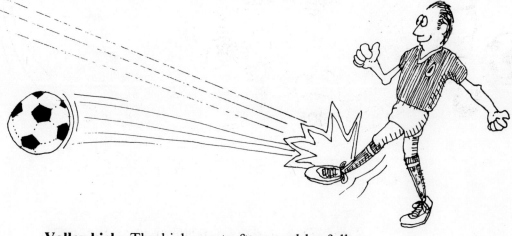

Volley kick—The kick most often used by fullbacks as a clearing kick. A well-executed volley kick sends the ball over long distances with height and accuracy.

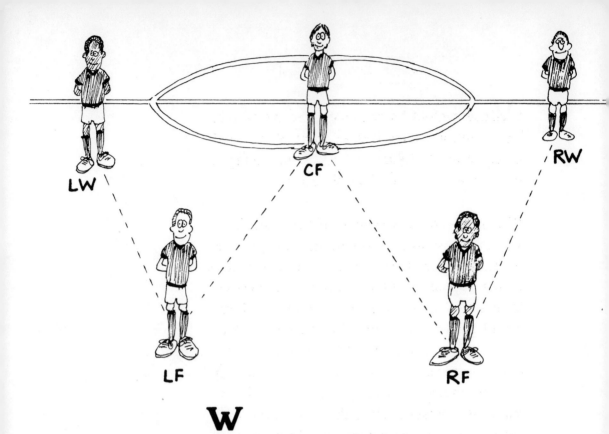

LW

CF

RW

LF

RF

W

W formation— A basic position pattern, the "W" formation describes the relative positions of forwards to each other.

Walking off the field— It is considered unsportsman-like conduct for a player to leave the field during play without the referee's consent.

Walking scrimmage— A practice game where players are allowed only to walk. Many coaches feel this slower type of play gives team members a chance to set up and run plays without being rushed into mistakes.

Wall (human)—A blockade of defensive players who position themselves in front of the goal in an effort to assist the goalie in saving a score in a direct free kick situation.

Wall pass—Soccer's version of "give and go." The wall pass usually occurs in a two-on-one situation, when there are two offensive players and one defensive man. The name was derived from street soccer, where an offensive player would get by a defender by angling the ball off an adjacent wall and then run past the defender to receive the rebound. In regular soccer, the offensive player passes off to a teammate, who passes back to the first player, who has run past his opponent into the clear.

Weak foot scrimmage—A practice game where each player is allowed to use only one foot to kick, tackle, or pass. The one foot used must be the player's unnatural kicking foot. This type of practice enables a player to develop skill and strength in his weaker foot without being at a disadvantage to opposing players.

Width—A term used to describe a team that takes advantage of the width of the field by spacing its players widely across it. By holding these wide positions, a team can take advantage of its set-up and establish a good passing game.

Wing halfback—Like the center halfback, the wing halfback must have confidence and ability in getting possession of the ball. He must also have knowledge and experience in knowing how to get it to his forwards. Offensively, the wing halfback supports his forwards in attacking maneuvers. In defensive situations, he pays particular attention to the opposing inside forward, always trying to steal passes or bottle them up.

World Cup—The Number One trophy in soccer. The World Cup match is held every four years and is open to any team in the world. The last World Cup tournament was held in 1974 in Mexico, when Brazil beat Italy in the finals, 4 to 1.

Y

Yellow card—If a referee feels that a player is displaying repeated unsportsman-like conduct, he gives that player a yellow card. This lets the player know that he is coming close to being ejected from the game.

Z

Zigzag formation—A practice formation where players line up in a zigzag pattern.

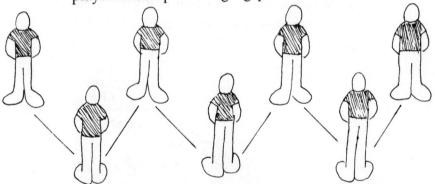

Zone defense—A defensive strategy where each player covers a specific area of the playing field instead of guarding one individual player.

A Few of Soccer's Greatest Players

Pele

His real name is Edson Arantes do Nascimento, and he was born in Brazil in 1941. He is considered by most to be the greatest soccer player of all time.

Pele played his first soccer game when he was 15 for a Brazilian team called the *Santos*. Making the most of a brief opportunity, he scored his first goal. After 1253 games and 1220 goals, Pele signed a contract with the New York *Cosmos* in August, 1975, that guaranteed him an estimated 4.5 million dollars.

No one thought that Pele would ever play for a United States soccer team, but the combination of money and the chance to help improve soccer in the United States was too good an offer to turn down.

Pele is the only player ever to play in three
World Cups and he is the first player to score
1000 goals. Indeed, his achievements are great.

Pele has been a driving force behind soccer
in the United States. He says, "You can spread
the word throughout the world, soccer has ar-
rived in the United States.

Kyle Rote Jr.

Kyle Rote Jr. is the United States' first
native-born soccer star. In his initial season

playing for the North American Soccer League's Dallas *Tornados*, Kyle was named Rookie of the Year.

His father, Kyle Rote Sr., was the Number One draft pick of the New York *Giants*. He played 11 brilliant seasons as a running back and wide receiver.

It was expected that Kyle Jr. would follow in his father's footsteps, and he did—for a time. In 1969, Kyle Jr. went to Oklahoma State to play football on a scholarship. During his spare time, he played soccer for enjoyment and as an exercise to keep in shape. Later he decided that soccer was a more enjoyable sport, so he transferred to the University of the South to play soccer—without a scholarship.

Rote graduated in 1972 and was immediately drafted by the Dallas *Tornados*. In his first season, he won the league scoring crown, and the word spread that Kyle Rote Jr. was going places.

Sir Stanley Matthews

As an indication of Stanley Matthews' ability as a soccer player and his excellent sportsman-like conduct, he was invited in 1965 to Buckingham Palace where Queen Elizabeth II named him Sir Stanley Matthews. He is the only athlete ever to receive this distinction.

Matthews is a small player, but he distinguished himself from other athletes by being a star at age 40 and by still playing with the best at 50.

Matthews joined *Stoke City,* an English team, when he was seventeen and later played with his favorite team, *Blackpool,* where the term "Stanley Mathews' Magic" was coined. The magic was his ability to outwit his opponents. One player said of him, "Trying to guard Sir Stanley Matthews is like trying to guard a ghost."

124

Eusebio da Silva Ferreira

Eusebio da Silva Ferreira has the deadliest kick known among soccer players. Born in 1943 in Portuguese East Africa, he reached the height of his career in the 1966 World Cup in England. Eusebio was awarded 1000 English pounds as a bonus for being the individual high scorer with nine goals in six games.

Eusebio once scored on 39 consecutive penalty kicks. When his string was broken, he congratulated the goalkeeper and asked him for his autograph.

Author JAMES B. GARDNER, a soccer enthusiast from early childhood, passes along his expertise and love for the game to today's young readers. This book, to a great extent, was stimulated by his travels in Europe and Central America where soccer is the major sport. Mr. Gardner, who is also a serious photographer, makes his home in Westchester County, New York. He is currently completing his undergraduate studies at Drake University (Iowa) School of Journalism.

DAVID ROSS is a talented sculptor as well as a creative artist. His sculpture has been exhibited at several upstate New York galleries including the Albright Knox Art Gallery and the Albany Institute of Art and History. A graduate of State University College at Buffalo with an M.A. in Educational Communications from SUNY at Albany, Mr. Ross currently teaches art in elementary schools in Saratoga County, New York, where he resides with his wife and their two sons.